The *Zen* of Travel

Wisdom from the Journey

LAINE CUNNINGHAM

The Zen of Travel
Wisdom from the Journey

Published by Sun Dogs Creations
Changing the World One Book at a Time
Softcover ISBN: 9781946732354
Hardcover ISBN: 9781946732361

Softcover Edition

Cover Design by Angel Leya

Copyright © 2017, 2018 and 2019 Laine Cunningham

All rights reserved. No part of this book may be reproduced in any form or by any means, electronic, mechanical, digital, photocopying or recording, except for the inclusion in a review, without permission in writing from the publisher.

Introduction

As the daughter of a military officer, I grew up on the move. By the time I entered college, I had lived in more than a dozen states. My family's longest stint, which spanned three years, was at an overseas post in Nuremberg, Germany.

After college, I continued moving around. A spiritual sabbatical that lasted six months was spent camping alone in the Australian Outback. My career has taken me from the West Coast into the Midwest, back to the Mid-Atlantic region, down into the Deep South, and out West. Canada, Portugal, Germany, Italy, and other countries have joined that list.

The journeys to, through, and from each place offered profound lessons. Regardless of the length of the stay, each trip changed my perspective about the world and myself.

This book has been distilled from those experiences so that anyone can achieve the enrichment offered by *The Zen of Travel*.

You will not be a local but you can enter the locale.

The journey to equals
the journey through.

Chase adventure so that adventure does not chase you.

*How far you go is meaningless.
How much you see is revelatory.*

Of all the things to pack, curiosity is key.

Instead of framing a photo, frame a memory.

The Middle English root of "travel" means "to strive."

Even a familiar location offers a unique experience.

A tourist transforms into a traveler.

Journey not by the map
but by your heart.

Art purchased during a trip always increases in value.

A change of place triggers change within.

Safety is a state of mind.

Even a short stay is a relocation.

The worst hotel becomes the home you make.

Returning home is also a pilgrimage.

Inviting others along also welcomes you.

Nomads carry only what is necessary.

The slower the pace, the greater the engagement.

To receive help,
ask.

Travel shifts more than the body.

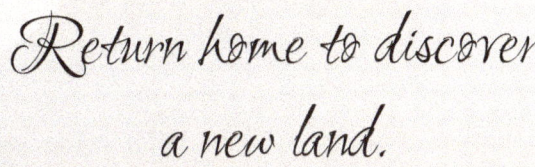

Return home to discover a new land.

Intelligent travel develops spiritual intelligence.

The closed mind never leaves home.

Know yourself to recognize the changes in your soul.

Those who miss you might not welcome the person who returns.

Greeting a stranger greets a friend.

Trusting is as important as knowing when to trust.

A favorite destination reflects the self.

Preparing for the trip prepares you for the journey.

Even the fragile butterfly wends a thousand miles.

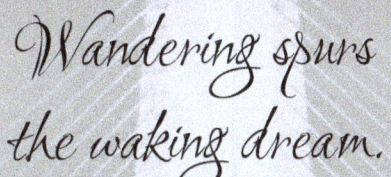

Wandering spurs the waking dream.

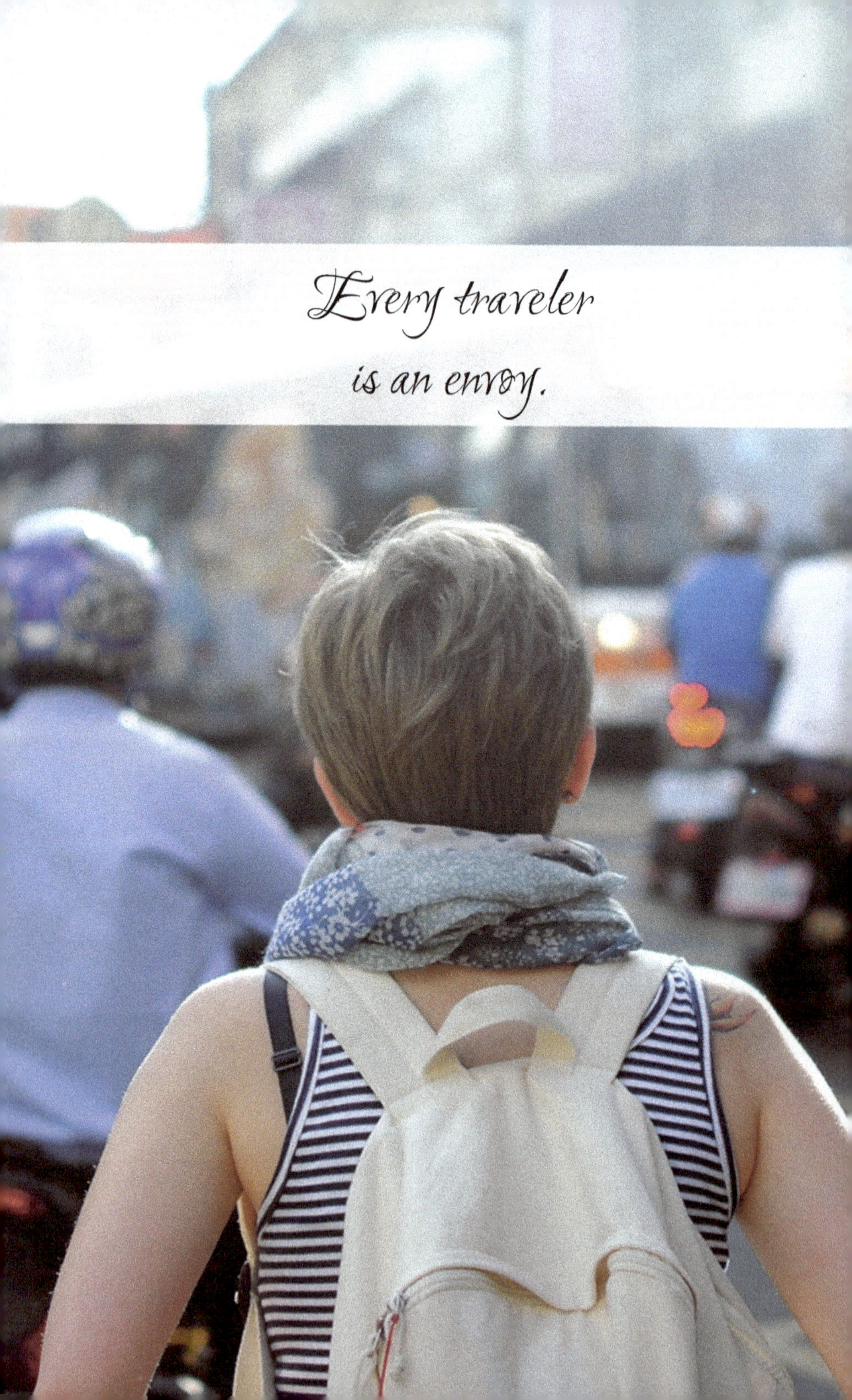
Every traveler
is an envoy.

You are responsible for all that you learn.

Travel revives senses that have slumbered.

Nothing matters except the journey.

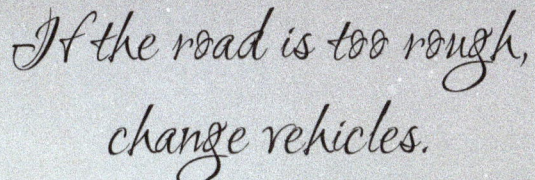

If the road is too rough, change vehicles.

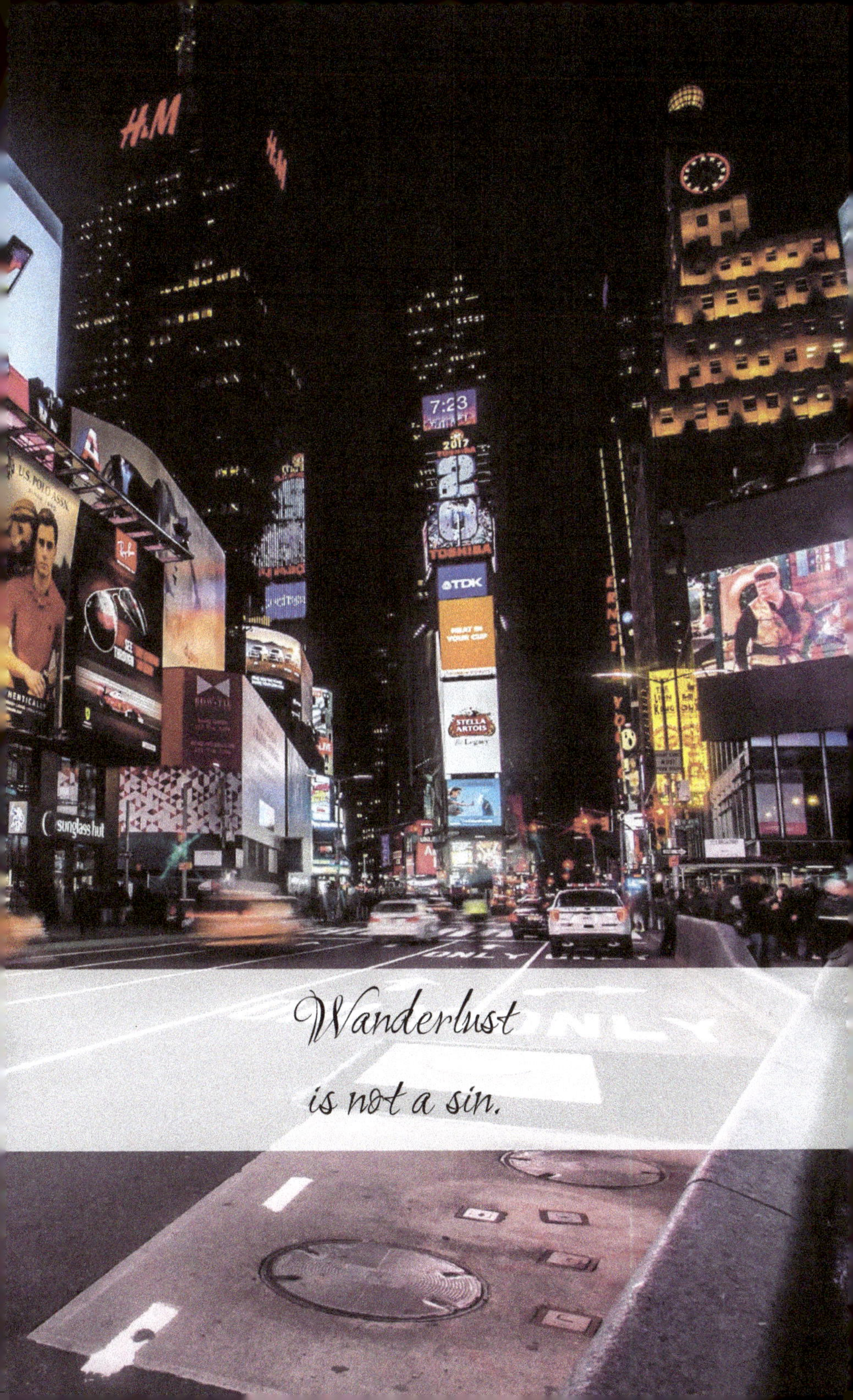
H&M
7:23
2017
TOSHIBA
TDK
STELLA ARTOIS
sunglass hut
Wanderlust
is not a sin.

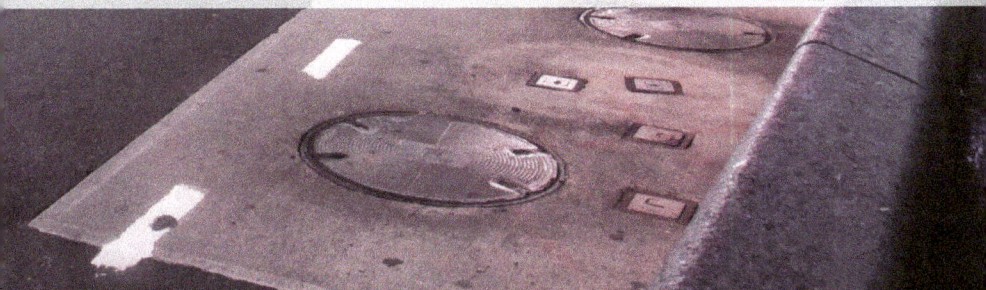

Vulnerability enhances intensity.

Short-lived pleasures taste sweeter.

Migration is more important than destination.

About the Author

Laine Cunningham's books take readers on adventures around the world. *The Family Made of Dust* is set in the Australian Outback, while *Reparation* is a novel of the American Great Plains. Her women's travel adventure memoir *Woman Alone: A Six-Month Journey Through the Australian Outback* appeals to fans of *Wild* and *Eat Pray Love*. Her work has received multiple awards including the Hackney and the James Jones Fellowship, and has been published by *Reed, Birmingham Arts Journal,* and the annual anthology by *Writer's Digest*. She is the senior editor of *Sunspot Literary Journal*.

Fiction

The Family Made of Dust
Beloved
Reparation

Nonfiction

Woman Alone
On the Wallaby Track: Australian Words and Phrases
Seven Sisters: Messages from Aboriginal Australia
Writing While Female or Black or Gay
The Wisdom of Puppies
The Wisdom of Babies
The Wisdom of Weddings

The Zen of Travel
The Zen of Gardening
Zen in the Stable
The Zen of Chocolate
The Zen of Dogs

Bikes of Berlin
Necropolises of New Orleans I & II
Ruins of Rome I & II
Ancients of Assisi I & II
Panoramas of Portugal
Nuances of New York
Glimpses of Germany
Impressions of Italy
Altitudes of the Alps
Knights Through the Ages
Utopia of the Unicorn
Portraits of Paris
Flourishes of France

www.ingramcontent.com/pod-product-compliance
Lightning Source LLC
Chambersburg PA
CBHW041959080526
44588CB00021B/2807